The Hay and the Barn

The Hay and the Barn

DAVID CRAIG

RESOURCE *Publications* • Eugene, Oregon

THE HAY AND THE BARN

Copyright © 2024 David Craig. All rights reserved. Except for brief quotations in critical publications or reviews, no part of this book may be reproduced in any manner without prior written permission from the publisher. Write: Permissions, Wipf and Stock Publishers, 199 W. 8th Ave., Suite 3, Eugene, OR 97401.

Resource Publications
An Imprint of Wipf and Stock Publishers
199 W. 8th Ave., Suite 3
Eugene, OR 97401

www.wipfandstock.com

PAPERBACK ISBN: 979-8-3852-0996-5
HARDCOVER ISBN: 979-8-3852-0997-2
EBOOK ISBN: 979-8-3852-0998-9

VERSION NUMBER 02/14/24

For Scotland, where I met myself a hundred times.

Contents

January 6—*Holy Hour.*	3
January 13—*Holy Hour.*	4
January 20—*Holy Hour. Flu.*	5
January 27—*Holy Hour (at home.)*	6
February 3—*Holy Hour.*	7
February 10—*I was giving the response: 'That we may be worthy of the merits of Jesus Christ.'*	8
February 23—*After Communion.*	9
February 24—*Holy Hour.*	10
February 26—*My Birthday.*	11
March 3—*Holy Hour.*	12
March 10—*Retreat. (My daughter's birthday.)*	13
March 17—*Holy Hour. (St. Patrick's Day.)*	14
March 24—*Holy Hour. The angel Gabriel's feastday.*	15
March 28—*After Communion.*	17
March 30—*In my bedroom.*	19
March 30—*Holy Hour.*	20
April 7—*Holy Hour.*	22
April 14—*Holy Thursday.*	23
Good Friday—	25
April 21—*Holy Hour.*	26
April 28—*En Route to Paris.*	27
May 12—	29
May 19—	30
May 29—	32
June 2—*Holy Hour.*	33
June 8—*Traveling.*	35

June 9—*At a "taking of the veil."*	36
June 10—*Anniversary of my first Communion.*	37
June 16—*Corpus Christi (As I awakened.)*	39
June 23—*Holy Hour.*	41
June 28—*From the garden came the exquisite notes of a blackbird.*	43
July 4—*After Communion I said to Him, "I'm most ashamed to think that You are placed on a useless and often unkind tongue."*	44
July 7—*I was thanking Him for the blessings He had given my neighbor.*	46
July 14—*(Bastille Day!)*	47
July 21—	49
July 28—*Holy Hour.*	50
July—*I was having great difficulty in accomplishing a work of charity.*	51
August 3—*After Communion (absentminded.)*	52
August 4—*Holy Hour.*	53
August 11—*Holy Hour.*	55
August 18—*There was a question of a surgical operation for me.*	57
August 25—	59
September 8—*At the hospital after an operation.*	60
September 15—*Convalescent. Holy Hour.*	62
September 22—*The priest came to hear my confession in my sickroom.*	64
September 29—*Convalescence.*	66
October 6—*I was trying to hold back someone who was being carried away by a terrible passion.*	68
October 13—*Holy hour.*	70
October 20—*Holy Hour.*	72
October 25—*(On the terrace.)*	74
October 27—*Holy hour. In my bedroom.*	75
November 3—*Holy Hour.*	76
November 10—*Holy Hour.*	77
November 17—*Holy Hour.*	79
December 1—*Holy Hour.*	81
December 8—*Holy Hour. Feast of the Immaculate Conception.*	83
December 9—*Feast day of St. Juan Diego.*	85

December 11—*End of the novena to the Immaculate. I was deeply moved by the Mass sung in five parts.*	86
December—*I was hearing of the enthusiastic remarks by readers of* Lui et *Moi (*He and I.*)*	87
December 15—*Holy Hour.*	89
December 22—*Holy Hour.*	91
December 29— . . .	93

Poems based on LUI ET MOI, 1949,
Gabrielle Bossis

Keynote: serve

JANUARY 6—*HOLY HOUR.*

"In life as in death, stretch out your arms to my All-Loving immensity. You see the picture—one going to meet the other. . . . Everything is possible in love. So come boldly."

Whose arms can reach, part the thin veils of death?
And yet it's by this that we will be measured—the breezes
that open our curtains. My body tells me it's coming.

Popes have made the trip, people more ripe
for the passage. "As in death," He says. Each day is the surprise
it brings: birds, a neighbor across the street, at his lawn.

Each moment is a mercy. Jesus is always revealing
Himself. And what have we ever had but praise—
for canyons, for my wife's dear face? (Yesterday, she said

she wanted me to live for two hundred years!) "In life,"
He says, though my husbandry skills have fallen dirt short;
the fruit, no doubt, of my sloth—though Jesus doesn't seem

to mind too much, His hand on billowing lace.
My wife and children are the only evidence I'll need!
I'll keen to leave them, will ask Him to keep their yearly

grief in His court. (They have opened me here—a cabbage
in this garden.) May His wounds widen, brighten both:
their sorrow, and those heavenly gates, with each passing year.

JANUARY 13—*HOLY HOUR*.

"What is lacking is loving desire for My glory—enthusiasm. . . . You lift
up your heads, but then you fall back on your self-center. . . . Long for
the fruit, so you may distribute it. . . . Your soul is only a little soul. Keep
it very simple. Discover and destroy."

Enthusiasm works best quietly, in the dark. Its rhythm
is slow, organic, like a kangaroo under a full moon.
He's the Divine Lover who slips beneath deep lake water,

without sound, much breath. You know those places—the fish.
(You can count on them! They rise with daytime temperature,
sink in cooling water, with crickets and the night.)

They could almost be that small friend from your youth.
Undersized, rounded, you never knew why the kid came,
though his silences were welcome. (And then later—in Lareto, Sligo!)

We can never walk with importance. How could we maintain
less? Joy's an empty cistern—Mary swimming
happily below that surface. She speaks Croatian.

And you're okay with that because You know
who gets the glory—Jesus. You can talk to Him
no matter how hot the day gets, no matter the confetti,

or how many people stand on cars. You don't know
this world, this one you walk on: empty, happy
parades, events which always fall short of the mark.

JANUARY 20—*HOLY HOUR. FLU.*

"You my brothers, continue My work. . . . Don't you think that at least three quarters of the people who do wrong fell into their way of life because they were not loved enough? . . . Acquire the delicate art of letting your neighbor feel that you stretch out . . . your heart to him."

—FOR MY DAUGHTER AND HER MATES

From the late shift parking lot, I watch one of my daughter's
hugely overweight warehouse co-workers, how her clumsy,
slightly stuttering walk might be a reaction to a lifetime

of parental wishes. Is she still walking through those,
(growing or not) wanting to affirm their good
or bad directives—moving with or against their expectations?

Is that why she twists herself slightly: a grown up child,
having gotten things largely wrong—or had they? How good
it would be if we could love better. (I could see the changes

that never happened!) Every one of us trudges northward.
That's how badly we need to get things right. Miracles,
survivors, surround us everywhere, work third shift.

I want to be like Jesus, to wash their feet in the rain.
I want my skin to know veils of morning mist.
I would move easier among all kinds of people.

My heart would be made of white ash, ripe blackberries.
I could skim down aisles, joking: sit in a fold-out
chair (in front of an opened car trunk) during lunch.

JANUARY 27—HOLY HOUR (AT HOME.)

"Are you sure that I alone count in your life and in your death? What means most to me is that my children give me preeminence in the life of the soul—this first life that they offer Me before their own, so that outside of Me nothing exists for them and they consider only their nothingness."

He's a winter lamb, a limb which shakes through snow.
He is darkness—a musical score that cannot close:
a Muslim hymn, the gaspings of bobbing, rain-drenched

spring petals. He's the power of first refusal. No voices
can intrude in His seasons. There are no puddled, icy
paths for us to take. He is only all,

don't you see, when He's not here; the bereft breath taken?
We do not matter. There is no neighborhood here.
(A cocked face, the raised eyebrow of a stranger.

That's all you can expect.) Each heaven has to disappear.
It's the undeniable completeness of this fallen world.
What you leave behind will be your only epitaph.

The need for mercy will form you. So cry out with birds,
with everyone you've ever let down. You stand, unfinished,
can supply no hope. You aren't ready for Eliot. Your environment

must complete its task, goad you into realizing what
you aren't. Come give your life to the darkness. (You can rest,
begin on old legs, have time, energy enough.)

FEBRUARY 3 — *HOLY HOUR.*

"Fan the flame of your confidence. Don't you need it along your way? Keep it burning in Me. I want you to be happy, so come back again and again to this feeling of trust until you are never without it. . . . Keep going blindly."

There's no other hand to grab, except the One
we cannot see. It's our best invisible bet.
(Money and fame are busy.) Come inside, where metaphorical

chandeliers brighten each hall! Our hope always flickers.
During the summer, an old veranda allows
for some second story ease, room away from the sway of trees.

Our lives are a-buzz with manners, faded wallpaper.
We're Confederate soldiers, articulate, anathema now,
people who don't belong. We had some generals,

some torn-up track that helped bring the truth back home,
here, where the sweet chains of Jesus, tradition,
are strong. The flies are real in this heat. An old

black man rocks hard on the porch. You can't know his song.
How could you, friend? You didn't know it then,
or now. (This is his plantation, too.) You can play

Happy Camper in your thrown-up tent with your pack of kids.
You pound in echoing stakes: the front yard, invite
passers-by to come in, recite some Tolkien, Tate.

FEBRUARY 10—*I WAS GIVING THE RESPONSE: 'THAT WE MAY BE WORTHY OF THE MERITS OF JESUS CHRIST.'*

"Shut yourself in and give Me the key. . . . My child, even the angels envy this beautiful life of ours—this oneness. Oh, this intimacy in time that leads straight to eternity. . . . What I want from you is a spirit of love and humility, one that is constant and independent from created things. . . . Joyously ready."

I find myself seated on a pile of broken bricks.
Rearranging them won't help. If I smoked a cigarette,
I could play the prince. A horse for my kingdom. Besides,

the sun might still come out. And who knows how
that could change us? The quiet could settle in:
happy trails of gauze, folding aloft in the sky;

sun, a country morning. You could walk out back,
bare-footed in the dew, with Jesus Himself, several
wax-sealed, stamped letters—your failures—under his arm.

One world is not the next! You sometimes rise up
like Lazarus, feel what it's like to be new in bed,
have a name in both places. How else could you possibly proceed?

The King is everywhere. There's no place to hide. These morning
birds can tell you that. (Someone else probably hears
them, too.) Time is limitless, friend, because heaven contains it.

It's a place where you can work, measure the slight bow
in each spiritual plank of wood. The world will call you
in for lunch, but the sandwiches do not come from here.

FEBRUARY 23—*AFTER COMMUNION.*

"You forgive Me for wanting you to be wholly Mine? I need all of your faculties as though they were necessary to My faculties as a man. Remember that I was a man among men even though I was also God.

"I need your acts of self-denial too, your discomforts and your bodily sufferings, just as though Mine were not complete..."

Heroism is, oddly, what we were born for, like birds
who risk every stage of nesting. There is no escape—
though you couldn't paint a finer world: the sounds

in the backyard, or front, life always asking for a little
more than we're inclined to give. Heroes aren't large.
They have names like Sally or Eunice. Their families eat corn

for dinner; they walk like lions into Dollar General.
What is necessary will come upon us, friend—as it
has always done. Our incompleteness surprises no one.

Such are the gifts of little people—and we
are all little people. (The saints go by,
tall, long-robed, gracing the sidewalks with heaven.

They bequeath us modest places!) We're street-sweepers,
though our attempts count as well. Each corner must
be squared off, our tools, put neatly back in place.

Help us, Lord, to cry out in our city sunset,
over beach fences, our ramshackled stucco houses.
We are ocean people. We know bare feet—and want.

FEBRUARY 24—HOLY HOUR.

"Above everything else, I want to do Your will."

"You see it is your first intention that gives a new color to your entire day, your entire life. Since you have this intention, be more trusting than ever, more certain than ever that God loves you. Isn't that magnificent? Nothing on earth can ever be compared with it."

The saints know how to hide in plain sight! They speak
a language that endures, a heart, staked down by desire.
That's why you could always hear my grade-school nuns

down the hall, their rosaries clacking, the swish of fabric!
It was 1964. God, I loved those women—
chalk circles for noses on the blackboard; leaning punishments

aside, they offered possibility, the only place
for this world. Every day they'd have another idea
on how to set us straight. It was generous, their thinking

about city kids. I loved how purposefully they moved.
(I should have followed.) They spoke cathedrals, sacraments,
wherever they walked. There was a rightness to it,

an ideal, a school for thought! And they didn't have to labor
their points. They set the ridiculous public schools straight,
put Rather, *Laugh In*, *Mad Magazine*, in their places.

Sister Mary Allen, door stop of heaven, I miss
your plain and wonderful face, your smile. You were
a voice worth listening to, especially when you struggled.

FEBRUARY 26 — *MY BIRTHDAY.*

"You will draw water joyously from the Savior's springs."

The shiny hats help to defeat the years.
"We scoff at endings! We celebrate you, a beginning,
the loveliness of what passes." (This is proof that we have no home here!)

We give boxed colors, ribbons: the temporal things
that must follow. Life itself is the confetti, the parade
—I remember, for my part, rigid brown-shirted Protestant*

Boy Scouts: two fingers to the "Be prepared" forehead—
the early sixties! So sure in their shallowness. (Jesus knows
about each party of leavers—sluggards and Ayn Rand

braving the foothills). Better to adopt this world!
The water gushing, never the same thing twice,
each fleeting configuration, a praise, a spring—with bells!

Your 40s friends knew Him because they knew you.
Angels attended your birthday, each fittingly attired,
because Life always manages to celebrate the coins of itself.

It spends itself in doing just that. Who has ever
felt lessened, after all, standing next to a spring?
Though numbered, who could add up the best of those days?

---

* *Many of our "separated brethren," no doubt, have their own stories.*

MARCH 3 — *HOLY HOUR.*

"Make it your first concern to be with Me. As though your roots, plunged into Me, would give the flowers and fruit of your actions a fragrance that would rise to your Christ.... When the end comes, what joy there will be for those who have tried to live only to please Me.... The end does come, and with the speed of a torrent that carries off everything at once.... I can look after everything.... Serve Me for the joy of serving Me."

Death never had any dominion. It was a dog
barking in a mist. Because hope is the city we live in:
with a lake, irises, delicate, a clearing that owns us.

And then You tell me this will end? You are why
it cannot, arms wide to gather or scatter birds.
And the saints, walking around downtown, in their meantimes!

They are always here at the cafes: hearts as clean
as occasional snow, with a goodness so elevated we hope
for contact—like paperboys in the Siena hills, our wagons,

stuffed with what's been half understood, behind
our little Doctor. She may yet teach us how
to swoon, like John—on the sweet fields of Your chest.

Everything I've wanted has always been wrong, because
the future cannot have my face. Heaven
contains earth, and more. It's the energy behind every movement,

time, thought, every prodigy. Our very passing
tells us we matter because we do—to you.
What could be better than that, You having Your way?

MARCH 10—*RETREAT.* (MY DAUGHTER'S BIRTHDAY.)

"If you but knew the power of a single elevated soul over my heart. Didn't I choose only twelve apostles to convert the world? Remember what I said, 'You are the salt of the earth.' So don't be timid when you speak of Me, but love one another with a love full of peace and great warmth. Isn't the life of God something that you share?"

Today, after adoration, attracted to the noise, beyond
two small windowed doors: the nave, I spotted a coffin.
I felt—was surprised by—a twinge of joy, relief.

And then this entry on my daughter's birth date! This
is an odd retreat. I wonder about the grief I'll feel—
the cumulative toll my passing will take on my best.

This is a new birth of faith—one that comes with death.
My family will still fly, as they were made to do!
My birthday girl—and her mother—who's been the land

I roam and love. (She's given my heart its season.)
Dear Bridget! She'll be in flower. I'll see her open—
though our talks will be different. Nothing important ends here!

That's what I'd want her to know. I'll be every river
she'll ever ride. Her life will still flap in its joy,
its absences. We've seen that, in the red cowboy hat

she wore as a child, in the jobs I've driven her to.
Like her mother, she's been a gift so large, it will take
heaven and all our friends to give it back.

MARCH 17—HOLY HOUR. (ST. PATRICK'S DAY.)

"Don't you feel new yearnings? The retreat is coming to an
end.... Open your eyes, your physical eyes and the eyes of your heart.
Have foresight and aspire with all your powers."

—FOR MY SON DAVID

We're always planning trips—to Kavanagh's Inniskeen!
(We'd secured a second semester in Gaming right before
we retired—in time for COVID.) This was David's fate

as a boy, so many awarded trips to Europe,
each eventually pulled, for one (often religious) reason
or another. God's always presenting, withholding; perhaps

that's how He deals with us excessive types.
May our only yearnings be for His designs! May the sun
shine on my son's double-wide. May all that doesn't

happen bring him joy. We learned about his autism
late. (I thought he was ignoring me and so I'd raise
my voice.... He once said I came on like a whale!) I wonder

what my own father would've taken back to help me?
We give those to Jesus; what else could we possibly do?
I try to ring bells when I see him. "I love you from here."

This is always a father's plight. We want to stand
upright, apart, to feel Him in a waking air.
(Maybe we'll find bagpipes to move him on our trip to Scotland!)

MARCH 24—HOLY HOUR. THE ANGEL GABRIEL'S FEASTDAY.

"Take a good look within yourself. Do you give joy to everyone you approach as the angel Gabriel did? . . . Do you weigh the word you would speak, the one you should withhold? Are you quick to do a favor? Are you full of loving enthusiasm for the glory of God? . . . Ask the Archangel to teach you to sing, to serve, to scatter joy—the joy that is God-Power. But ask often. . . .

"Oh, My little children, what a grace faith is. . . . You who are rich, give to the poor."

My Down's son sings on his bed, ear-phones in,
YouTube engaged; his laughter has a busyness to it.
Perhaps he's impersonating a hero as he earnestly waves

a sock in each hand. He's what I know of angels!
Who else sings heaven, so close at hand? He offers
often a surprising generosity. (His sister has, by now,

replaced his married older brother as model, mage.)
Who more richly faces each morning: "What we doin' today?"
He teaches me, each time I cannot make out

what he's saying. My wife is the same, really, in her
oblique ways. What can I grasp of either? And when
I drive my daughter to work, what new neuro-pathways

do we widen? This is the foolishness we're born to, an angelic
sign-language, one we never completely learn.
St. Michael doesn't mind, rocking on the balls of his feet.

It's how Jesus teaches us love. He throws up a Walmart pizzeria. (And me, a tall weed in cracked asphalt! I bob, crooked, unengagingly, a startling blue.)

MARCH 28—*AFTER COMMUNION.*

"When He shall come to judge the living and the dead. . . . But now is the time of great mercy, and I come to love. Above all, live this present moment." *(My mind was going back to the past on into the future.)*
 —For the woman on Facebook who said we lose too much from childhood. We can never, she claimed, start an adult conversation with, "Look, I found this rock. Doesn't it look like a potato?"

How much future did Gabrielle have? She dies the next year, surrounded, no doubt, by flowers. She strewed her own grave with them before she went. The nice word here,

following a garden newt there. Jesus expected
as much! It was a providential march, her winters, springs;
this riot, always in present tense. Our days,

too, must add up to little. (Our pies must be round,
crimped.) This is where children live—where friends are so fast
that they don't always remember your name. And you *can* tell

an adult that you found a rock that looks like a potato!
Immediately the two of you would be as thick as thieves!
How could one not respond to that? It'd be

like third grade all over again. (Gabrielle* could play,
after all; she loved dramatic immediacy. May
she pray us into today!) This is heaven's way,

She was an actress.

full of beautiful culverts, ankle turns. Jesus
walks here. We discover His world as He invents
the first flugelhorn. We're the first person to find it, try it out.

MARCH 30—*IN MY BEDROOM.*

"My child, ponder more often on the value of the present moment, the danger of going back over the past and the uselessness of gazing into the future. Just give the little moment that you hold in your hands. Simply and lovingly."

The present is the only neighborhood where you can't find answers. It's the beat-up playground down your street, the faded color of the swings. It's where other people really are.

Their spontaneity puts you in your place, where the bluest skies can clear! You can only be real in the present—where your losses own you. It's the basketball hoop we give to Jesus.

No one with a name or reputation lives here! The clothes you wear—are worn. The present, like humility, has an imperfect face: yours! Anything happens all the time.

Life is (and like) a prayer, the little we can give.
(At night, the moon and stars help as you walk back, past the garage: those two close deer my dog barked at,

lit up in my neighbor's spotlight. They were as surprised as I.) The present, friend, is the great equalizer. Nobody's rich in the present. We all move, naked,

like we were at birth, our lives as they happen. It's the only place where God can blink. Our life's tight bud powers open. (Go ahead, we say, break open a new deck.)

MARCH 30—*HOLY HOUR.*

"Take note of your thoughts. Don't you see that they occupy the greatest part of your existence. They belong to an interior realm you must learn to rule since from them comes what is worthy and unworthy in your days. Keep them constantly in the climate of God, of His glory, His will, His mercy, and all the qualities that make Him what He is.

". . . Don't believe in chance, but learn to see the hand of your Father, your friends—the one who never leaves you—in everything that happens."

Three doinking Stooges, poking each other as if God
depended upon their rectifying insight: old flags,
bagpipes. Yet they hardly know where, or how to stand—

on what ground. They're like Tuesdays, the horn of justice blowing
at work, points scored for the local deserving man:
our midrash, commentary, the verdict no one has asked for.

Bruises need to be healed so we can rule, or at least
enjoy our stay. One version of me wears an eye-patch,
in another I stand in this drunken boat, Li Po

or Rimbaud, in the vestiges of my won quiet—at last,
glitter, the everything I deserve! But . . . no, they're at it
again, poking eyes, throwing pies at taller women.

We can only hope they'll weary of the hair (or the lack
thereof), that they'll learn to clam up a little, realize
that God has accounted even for, orphaned, them.

Silence has always been our home—in no good condition.
Jesus patches the old place, even as it survives our rage.
We wait outside for our ubers, no excuse in the world.

APRIL 7—HOLY HOUR.

"Why should you be astonished at having a soul ordained of God since I, your brother, am the eternal Priest? . . . You have a share in everything I am.

"Surrender yourself to the Father as if you had received the indescribable sacrament or ordination, knowing that you belong utterly to God."

Swinging a censor, I wonder what I'm doing here?
These clothes are foreign—a gold, stiff chasuble (little house)!
I don't exist, can't, when I extend my hands.

There's no waking up from this. I reach, and the world
is, therefore, changed. He does this every day.
(Broadcast news might be next!) Jesus, what

have I ever understood? You come, a King, bring a life
that matters. I'm new. How could it be otherwise?
This gold defines us. I'll have it on when I stop

at Clerkenwell or Putney. (By appearances they will know us.)
That's why we're forever waiting, among our betters.
Will I have to live in a new foreign place? Will I learn

its manner—and so, perhaps, become less of a priest?
Better to feel the charge of a difference, bequeathed;
to be in over my head. May people always see

what I'm not. May the guise own me, like Catherine's Siena,
so drunk in heart that she (and it) could barely stand—
or a young man wearing a gold he cannot sustain.

APRIL 14—HOLY THURSDAY.

"Stay very close to me today. Today is the day of great love. Celebrate its anniversary in your simplest, most affectionate way. See love first. Give love first. Seek love first, and you'll fulfill my desire for you. . . . all the rest is nothingness."

"Have you ever thought of the burden of love that made Me institute the sacrament of the Holy Eucharist. . ."

"What language must I speak to make you understand Me? If your faith is too weak to find burning words, ask Me to speak to Myself in you. . . . Place your heart between My fingers as a harp with its string tuned and stretched. I'll make music that will ravish earth and heaven. Would you like to be that instrument again?"

"Oh Father, we give you thanks . . ."

Gesture becomes act. We eat our God, who eats
the leaves, burning up in the fall. He's the calloused hands
which hold each flower! His apostles, after all, had weight,

number. Like well-used harnesses, heavy with sweat,
they spelled out their world—like today in West Virginia:
two out-back horses, alone, muddy, their coats thick

with drying holler dirt, their small-pen hooves, mucked
in standing water. They loved us as we slowed, driving.
(My Downs' son sometimes thinks I'm daft, talking

Jesus to horses, but there's that other part of him, too,
who assents.) "This is My body"—the hills, animals.
This is the good price we have to pay. Francis

fools: the Bread, which is Jude's accompanying slide whistle;
It's the silence that owns us. (Or the earthquakes that have to come.)
Each molecule heating in a Love which transforms Itself.

"This is the Bread," He says, "breaking, always breaking."
These are the fingers the Word uses to create sound,
a you, plucked, ripe enough to feel each sin.

GOOD FRIDAY—

"Why should you use long sentences and difficult words to speak to
Me? Just talk with the utmost simplicity as you do with your family and
intimate friends. I belong to the inner circle, don't I?"

This is not a happy door. Blood on the knob,
dark wind once you open it; dust swirls. You're outside
with the cries of women. We have to go there whatever

we believe—deaths, relationships that go south. We know
contorted mouths, the mat of hair. There's no getting
around this love business. And though we will never

probably know nails, or have a following, some days
will feel like this. We won't want to play. But we will.
We will sit on that hill. God's feet will offer no consolation—

as He hurls His pulp back against the wood,
as He tries to get air. It's all blood, to the end of Him.
He will cry out in a language we do not know.

Then the show will end. We've got our own lives we can't
get the better of. This will follow us to the water cooler.
Someone I love will be in a deadly place,

and I'll pay for my involvement. That person will make
us human because this struggle is larger than we are.
Maybe they'll have Down's or autism. Our love can't save them.

APRIL 21—HOLY HOUR.

"Today you wanted to live with My loving-kindness. Keep it by you all day long. Adore it. Love it. Let it be your very gentle companion, so that those around you feel the effects of it. Express it by smiles full of goodness. Try to judge no one today. Say all the good you can about others and don't mention their faults."

—TV AT TEN YEARS OLD

His mansion is a better one to live in. The air currents
have room enough to eddy, back to front.
The trees outside spike our days with a flush of leaves.

It's late May in a temperate zone. Here our faults don't exist,
or aren't worth the notice. It's a kind of bizarro-world—
really, since I'm always new to the place. Still, changes

are good. (It's like I'm driving with Jude again: thirty
or so piglet butts, running in front of our car
down a shaded backwood county road.) Every home

here is backwoods. We could raise a company of capable men,
here, under clear skies. It would be like building
your own cabin, playing Davy Crockett, or Fess Parker.

They solved every case at a preferred distance, little talk.
It might've been enough to get you to become a mason,
because simplicity draws, the kind every congressman

from Tennessee, with a 60s tv filter, should possess.
With coonskin cap, I learned to be laconic, my legs,
too short, finally—though Texas walked with everyone.

APRIL 28—*EN ROUTE TO PARIS.*

"Think often about Me, My little girl. Think often.... Your free will with all its opportunities will no longer exist in heaven, you understand?... A thought is a soul's glance. Let yours be warm, natural, frequent...

"Believe that everything in your life is arranged expressly for you...

"May this look at Me form as it were a divine being in you...

"Then be saturated with Me in My life on earth where you can follow Me.... Your earthly life will not go on much longer. Make haste to join Me...

"Be your Christ for others."

My life often feels like a train ride to Paris. Someone
keeps calling out the wrong stops. I don't recognize the scenery,
the out-of-date collars these people wear. I just

bump along. (My oldest friends, gone.) Who knows what
will happen next? Who knows what kind of Paris
could rise up? Perhaps a smaller town, one beneath

ornament, gesture. People might come out as they are.
(It would be like showing up at one of Kavanagh's
dance halls, everyone local enough to fit in.)

We can find comfort in the tracks that move beneath us,
talk to people. Then toast, grinding the grains
against our buttered molars. Can one dance on a train?

Yes, if you'll willing to allow for the rocking, can change
partners. (I try to teach my daughter this!)
Earth was made for the living. Everything is here:

the laughter, the ease—if you're willing to get bumped a little,
off rhythm. We dance with His will, our faulty steps.
Our sweat, not so secretly, wants to name only Him.

MAY 12—

"When you come to Me, come quickly, with that warmth that is the heartbeat of love. If you are slow, if you find it difficult to tear yourself away from what you are doing where is the joy of love, where is its eagerness?"

Birds bring each morning. Solitary, hopping the wet walk
out back next to the garage. It's conducive: a new day
always brings more rain than you might expect. They all

start out this way! That's why it's an advantage to get up
under a cloak of silence. I catch the wind
before my family, can move like the octopus I saw

on educational tv, spindling my tentacled way
across the silent tank, my cups speaking a new language.
How else can I name that light in my ocean window?

Wasn't it Catherine from Siena who said that we are octopi;
God, the water! (A constant baptism!) This day,
like the later morning trees out back in the distance,

high up, how leaves circle in fierce, wet successions
of tossing limbs, neighborhood trees! They offer
too much movement, as life does, a kind of apocalypse.

The scenes, the winds, the grief in those boughs, might overwhelm us. But we have God to come back to, this Ground
we're always wandering away from—even in sleep.

MAY 19—

"Do you think that you could keep going very long without Me? Don't you feel you should cry out your need to Me? Don't you understand that I need this cry of yours?

"I am here with treasures. If you don't ask Me for them, how can I give them to you? If you didn't tell Me often that you love Me, where would be my joy?"

—LUKE 7: 11–17

We sink, I suspect, because some part of us needs
to move our hands along life's deepest rock faces,
the pools of the dead. It's where we must grow, relearn

who we are! There we, seeds, earth-husks, can begin
to dig, crack open our creases. In what sunlight comes,
we can feel God's pale hand uncoil, start to scour.

Angels stand back, reverence each split, each need.
And soon a twisted protuberance finds air—an earthen
stick-baby-to-be. (Life is its only reward!)

That's why we celebrate our pain, croak the word—Love.
Growing, we try our own surfaces. We set new faces
against ancient ruins, rain. We must feel that sheath

behind us as it clings, drags. Like an old hat,
it pulls before shriveling in its death. We cry out our names
(learning them)! Let us be that to You,

a sound which only knows it can never understand.
We're citizens, again in this reading, of an unknown town—
this rising green. We meet the futures we contain.

MAY 29—

"Do you know what I'm going to ask you today? To learn to speak of
the good in others. It's a sublime habit. What an example you would
set! . . . Would you like to try today and go on trying all through your
tomorrows until your death?"

It's a holy handkerchief on a wound—to draw up the good:
like broth from a bone! It's insisting on heaven, something
beyond us. How hard it is to live as if goodness

endures! It's seems like Pollyanna's glad hand, the lining
that defines every gray cloud. It's an end we insist on!
But only because It came here first. So say

something nice! You'll be in the vanguard. They pass out little hats!
The Knights of Columbus will follow you down the street,
swords held high. They'll scurry, want you to walk

beneath their erratic silver tent. I'd pull
away; give me a small neighborhood five
and dime beneath an El instead, maybe

in Brooklyn. There are people there too, where opportunities
abound. Good news travels fast in the city,
after all. I might even make new friends, though that

would pass. A good word, though, bears each moment, remakes
us all. Those days, then, are changed, in God's
second school. And the world is not what it was before.

JUNE 2—*HOLY HOUR.*

"Don't you have the impression that you still think of Me as being the distant and severe one? Smile when you speak to Me, believing that this makes me happy. And if you think of the joy you give Me, won't you come closer and more happily to Me, as though you were in My heart?

"You see, you mustn't expect happiness from the things of the earth, but solely from your way of communing with God."

". . . Let your love flow out to meet My tenderness. It will be the repetition of the first symphony heard by God and Adam."

You could say He's the arch on a bridge, and you wouldn't be wrong—
or winter's knotty woods off a backwoods road.
God is happy there, in big, wet boots, some kind

of civil war overcoat. (He watches Ken Burns in a cabin.)
Sorrow's always on the way somewhere—it's not
an end-stopped deal. Take your silences in a car, for example,

when you're driving alone. He's an able navigator, arms folded
(as distant as you are). You can share whatever's on your mind;
rain, by then, could be beading, running along

and down your side windows. His mother's there too,
no surprise, in the back seat, clicking her knitting needles.
The two of them choose to stop and stand out in the rain—

against some dumpster, next to a rural store.
(She keeps knitting.) The water waddles down the Master's face.
"I made this, you know," He says. "It's like life sometimes,

no one there to give you the song." Then He turns and steps
deeper into wet woods. Cinching her hood,
Mary turns, blinks at you (for humor), smiles through the water.

JUNE 8 — *TRAVELING.*

"Of course it gives Me more pleasure when you come to Me in the crowds than when you are alone in your room. The crowds in Paris leave Me alone as though I were still dead."

The Metro could break down, become a meeting place.
The city: homeless, finally! Fall on your knees,
great city! It is the poor who gather in forgotten fields,

who bring you mercy. Even in a downpour, we have
this choice. Jesus is not dead. (And who says you have
to be at the front of a line?) Gather your losses;

they are a new species of flowers, planted in heaven.
Keep walking, until you reach the end of your meadow.
(We all carry our sins, the street of Paris; after all,

we laid them there—heavy stones, hard to lift—
unwillingly, in a kind of line!) St. Francis did something
like this. He doesn't mind helping again. He'll bring winter,

where crowds can work the Jungian darkness. The person
next to you is the gate you'll need. Eternity
will move in his hands, wounds! It's our place among

the crowds of the dead. (Others play games in the night:
kicking decapitated human heads, snatching corpses
for medical experiments. The corporal works of mercy!)

JUNE 9—AT A "TAKING OF THE VEIL."

"See the simplicity of love in everything, even in the very little things. Why shouldn't the little things be as precious as the big ones if they belong to your love-life?"

—FOR MY THREE-YEAR-OLD GRANDSON, JOSEPH

It's the buzz the fly moves in, the veil nuns take.
It's the incompleteness of our joy. We see that the answer has never been enough! We rise only in the telling. He becomes

the clothes we wear, the long face we have
to splash away above our morning bowl.
How else could we bring enough? A three year old

may want to engage in some serious play today!
(The thin wires of regret will not help you with him!)
You appear only to love, to carry the rhinoceros

horn. That is why you've joined this order of unlikely
contemplatives. Faithfulness is always accomplished in the quiet:
Joseph in Arimathea, collecting the body, the linen;

Pilate; the Mary who sat in the elements outside.
Who wouldn't choose that role, the calm each one of them walked?
(It would be morning. It would be first century Palestine!)

The sun will rise when you get yourself up today.
You'll realize, again, that you belong to Someone Else.
This is where Life is: when day begins to take over.

JUNE 10—ANNIVERSARY OF MY FIRST COMMUNION.

"When I give Myself entirely it is for always—unless I am refused. Then do you find it surprising that I want you in your offering of each little moment of your lives? If we are everything to one another all the time, we have great joy and nothing can take it from us.

"My life was spent entirely for others. I loved and I saved. You child, love and save the honor of My name of Savior.

"Win souls. Work for souls. Prayers, yes, but also sacrifices."

A public intimacy—the only hall of heaven.
Each pew noise marked us: suited kids for Jesus.
This is where my mother, father, first heard their names!

Angels bowed, a new world had been created, though I
was too young to know. So what do I do with that now?
(That always remains to be seen.) I could stand before meals,

take less, say "For one soul." I don't remember
what I would have said to this back then, though I folded
my hands correctly, pointed my fingers. Combed up

in the late 50s, eight, waiting for my Answer:
there was one in that suit, in black and white; a place
in time, recorded, because my parents had an inkling

in their own lives. Life always seemed so provisionally
given, even with our "yes"s. Still, there was time,
an order which would have us. It brings these things back.

Because what life wants to give less than all?
Each day, the things we've left undone, or done poorly,
forever can change. We're left with that suit, that child.

JUNE 16—*CORPUS CHRISTI (AS I AWAKENED.)*

"Happy Feast Day, my dear God."
    "You know, there need not be any interruption between
Corpus Christi on earth and Corpus Christi in heaven. The procession
never stops. The last Altar of Repose is in heaven—the heart of God
where my blessed ones live. So begin right now to sing and thank and
adore. . . . Take a moment to love Us better. To talk to Me about yourself,
above all about your weaknesses."

We walk in heavenly procession. (There is no careful
periphery.) A boy stops to stoop, pick a flower.
Nobody need wait. Everywhere is the altar of repose,

where even the guilty bear the glint of love.
They've sailed sudden ships of sighs to get here.
And while earth today might deliver a shank of weather:

high tides and tumbling corn, this will still be our prayer—
Jesus, help me to paint a bluer sky,
help me to be like Mary, not an ounce of self

consciousness. She was so quiet—no one noticed!
Who else could move the Pacific Ocean, the harbors
where each beat ship must be rebuilt, the skies,

corrected, in the sounding of hammers, hoisted canvas,
men's voices—where the lumber, labor, and libations are free?
Tennyson might play his epic pipes on deck,

reach for what he can never have, as the sea,
sun, become a kind of paten, raise him up.
Every sea bird processes, every weakness finds its sail.

JUNE 23—*HOLY HOUR.*

"You and I together, we make only one.

"It is time to see Me in a new light—the powerful light of reality.

"Even when you are doing the most ordinary things I am with you, because while I am the greatest, I am also the humblest, and nothing is ever deadly dull to Me. What is more obscure and despised only attracts Me more."

Sister Mary Allen stalked her sorrow. (I called,
years later, but she couldn't place me, bound by old students—
ones who seemed to have plied emotional or monetary scams.)

This was after she'd left the order; but I'd seen her there,
in front of us eighth grade kids, every day, how she always
gave more than the lesson, in her habit; the way hidden ones

proceed: in the creases, in the fabric. She was the model
whom no one ever noticed, at least at first. (I remember
the sound of those glorious, over-sized waist beads in the hall.)

Whatever my errant ways, those nuns didn't change—
even the ones we threw Milk Duds near, on our high
school's cafe stage. (It morphed into our first food fight.)

Such is the price for drama, for helping others!
But Sister, whatever happened for you, you gave
me that. You showed me how to lay myself down.

And so we follow, quietly, in the recesses of our lives—
at least often. What a trail of misfits You managed to lead!

(Something good happened that lunch period: a boyhood camaraderie!)

JUNE 28—*FROM THE GARDEN CAME THE EXQUISITE NOTES OF A BLACKBIRD.*

"You know why he's singing so sweetly? Is it because the sky is blue? No, it's because he's answering another."

—FOR J. BOTTUM

We always get it backward. Falling leaves
invite the wind, the song spells out its name.
The bird calls its mother, who calls her dearest Friend,

the sweet echoes we are, that we become.
We need a robe from Palestine to walk this road.
We need the voice of the women. Blackbirds bring

the earth they sing, the trees, the sky, the absent
boy who once walked beneath. (The world, here, is
an expression of love!) Like that song, a grieving post

of an almost-friend: "I heard the voice of Jesus
say," the sylvan-placed Celtic sorrow of a man
who'd just lost his long-suffering wife. On Facebook. The world

is filled with extraordinary people. Give me light for this day.
Let me be like a leaf on a summer tree, knowing
too little—the feel of rain. A season will come

and break off my stem. Let me know that place is this:
the life-giving stream. Our wives, the voices in that green.
May they take us before we're gone. We follow after.

JULY 4—*AFTER COMMUNION I SAID TO HIM, "I'M MOST ASHAMED TO THINK THAT YOU ARE PLACED ON A USELESS AND OFTEN UNKIND TONGUE."*

"I know it but I come all the same. Even when you don't believe in My grace, I give it. . .

"Oh, precious faith! Use every manner and means of increasing it. Seek it as one who beams a light into dark, unexplored corners. Faith is what brings the Creator and the creature in touch with each other. And when you have affirmed all the powers of your faith, your hope and love increase to tighten the bonds of union."

—for Fr. Jim Blount, SOLT

Double-wide, a box of chicks under a shed's heat lamp.
That's the uncouth way He comes, in a son's setting—
like a friend who wears out-of-fashion madras shirts.

Why be embarrassed? He's the truest thing you've seen.
You can go anywhere with the guy. And he's so friendly—
waitresses, charmed, get taken into the fold.

He leaves generous tips, likes Frank Sinatra and wooden
baseball bats. He could live in City Park.
The only parties he goes to are there—where birds

flutter up, stones flat across the pond. Skyscrapers
still amaze him, as does every human invention: molded
dashboards, the thought that creates a steering wheel!

(He could be an innocent, this priest, inciting miracles,
a man raised up since childhood to do his job.
You will never hear his name on the news, real

or Catholic. He embarrasses when he talks about angels, forty
feet high. But how else would you expect this to go?)
His life's just a stone's throw from here. A big one.

JULY 7—*I WAS THANKING HIM FOR THE BLESSINGS HE HAD GIVEN MY NEIGHBOR.*

"Many times, a thought from one of you is a cry, and I listen to it. Oh, cry often so that I can answer you, My very little ones. My Benjamins all down the centuries, believe in your Listener so much that you give thanks even while you are asking, and everything will be done to give you the joy that you yourselves have given Me."

Look at yourself as the tenderest of shoots. Much of you
has not yet happened. We have such a meager concept
of leaf and burl! (Doesn't dirt knock you out, as it roughs

up your palm?) This is fitting. An army can have only
so many Davids, Goliaths. Surely, there've been
other times when you weren't the chosen one. No one

expects it of you—anymore. (If they ever did.)
This, too, is in keeping. He's the thanks that comes, hand
in hand! And this is the little given house we live in.

(The neighbors who live next door are the speech of God!)
We ask for what we need—no one else pays attention.
Each request is small part of Your plan! This morning

I read about You passing the first apostles by the sea;
your choice allowed them to participate. That was how they came
alive. (You're gentle as a horse in a recessed field,

a blinded one, silk covering its morning eyes from flies!
What can we do but sit next to You on slightly
dew-damp sod, turn our faces to warm in the sun.)

JULY 14—(BASTILLE DAY!)

"Ask Me for this hunger for Me. It will increase your zeal in the service of your God. Can you evoke the name of God without a feeling of mysterious charm? What perfection could be lacking? Then what can you not expect from Him? And if you depend on God for everything, never cease to call Him so that He may act and speak in you as the tone of a bell, the breath of a flute, or the vibration of a hard string."

—FOR SAM SHEPARD

This is how Jesus sounded when He sent the crowds back home.
Like us, they returned to the same hovel, self;
maybe they moved the furniture around, or walked fields.

Later, they could hear the Spirit ruffle bare bushes;
what He didn't say would come back at the end of the day,
crackle in the hearth. . . . They felt the distance between

Him and a bare hook on a row of them.
They'd squat by Sam Shepard's fire, wonder about
all that was missing, no words across porch rot.

Give us more of that absence, Lord, that abscess, give us
the hunger of everyman. We live at the bottom of the spiritual
food chain. Sam has relayed those stories, family

scraps that mar us: the lone wolf, now on stage,
clans gone so wrong that everybody recognizes themselves.
Need sets up camp off-Broadway, in New York City.

It's the screams that literally save us—. There are no lies,
after all. We get exposed. The wounds of not-saints,
in the glare of staged lights, in the darkness that follows.

JULY 21—

"You believed in the affection of your mother and father. Then believe
in Mine; I am both Mother and Father. . . . Imagine My joy when you
believe as I want you to believe! . . . You know that I pay attention to
what you ask Me. Even before you speak My ear is against your lips. . . .
   "What a beautiful loss to be lost in Me, never to find yourself
again! Since I enfold you, don't hunt any further. You've arrived."

That was a First Communion we could stand on, in place.
That moment was, as it turned out, enough:
my mother and father insisting on my saintly future.

What part of any gift comes back empty? (The packaging!)
Everything else must keep changing: galaxies,
the Horsehead Nebula. They reconfigure what Praise means

to Itself. Don't you feel that when you dip your hand
into a stream? Or in early summer breezes, under
now completed leaves? This is what it means to arrive

(though it will take awhile for our baggage to catch up!
The airport is busy.) My parents knew this: that's why
they gave us edges to sharpen our childhood's wares.

It's like that this morning, as my daughter starts a new job.
Let my prayers be like some crazy stairs You build—
to You. She'll never guess its lean, how clean

the gold. There will be those days when she sits in the night,
stars her only companions. The stairs will rock
a little, sigh. (This will be how she'll know she's home.)

JULY 28—HOLY HOUR.

In my bedroom in the country.
"I didn't leave you during the thirty-three years of My life nor throughout eternity. Then may I not ask you never to leave Me deliberately, to stay with Me right to your last moment on earth, that moment of our meeting? How well you will understand then that to quicken your heartbeats you had to hold Me closely in your very breathing."

As close as two breaths can be to being one,
we would cling to heaven, always a catch away!
(I wait to open Your eyes—with mine. That's how

my passing life will get left behind.) May heaven
insist, invade. May her troops wade in, take the
sun-drenched shore! You'll sit right there in the last

hospital, everything hanging in its usual balance.
We'll try to do what we can to make Your world
more apparent to loved ones. (The sins that would've crushed me

will eventually fall in ruin, rusted in some field,
strewn about—ancient failed and wasted machinery!)
How strange will Your hand be then, Your fingers in mine.

Let them be so now. My hand, which I'm getting to know
will soon be gone—finalized. Who will find me,
though no one will need to. My heart, like today, will reach

after some bird. I will find me, my head on Your shoulder, my feet,
waving Your mercy in the delicate voices of a stream.
(I have coins for the trip, everything just a mile away!)

JULY—*I WAS HAVING GREAT DIFFICULTY IN ACCOMPLISHING A WORK OF CHARITY.*

"Don't you want to begin to be happy to suffer a little for Me?"

"Help someone." Pain, my unwelcome friend!
We're never finished until we are! It's a mistake
to fool ourselves about this. Suffering opens

us up to the whole of our lives. (Wide-hatted, calm,
she works, like grandma, in the soil of her garden. Her wrinkles,
smiles deep, abide. Never pressed for time, she carefully

spades, turns the soil. You don't recognize the song
she's humming.) We'll try to be grateful for the only gift
we can give: our forgettable lives. Let it be for someone

else (for a change). She'll linger, stay for as long
as you need her to. And who knows, maybe you won't have
to endure so much—since canonizations are set aside

for those better prepared. Your will will depose itself
in an extended sigh: our second last prayer! The last one,
deeper still, will lead us home. Pain will lift us.

our bodily weight, as we begin to leave
our individually-wrapped concerns; the flesh will let go
after all these years, no one left to set it adrift.

AUGUST 3—AFTER COMMUNION (ABSENTMINDED.)

"I'm here." *(In a tone of gentle reproach.)*

Maybe her shoes felt tight. Maybe she detected
a curious tightness in her hip. We're like the child,
looking for a single reason to behave in the pew.

Attention is a bird of the will. But there's so much
to be said for the beautiful world outside: oddly
colored birds, white rails, silver nails, in the blue. That's why

this Soft Voice from another place! A large kneeler
noise behind us; then the Eucharistic elevation brings Him
back home, though we wonder why life should take effort at all—

it's so nice over there. Thankfully, the chasuble, the chalice
lets us know that God is here, too. And not. (Your childhood
will save you; though it won't set you free.) That's why you're at
    Mass:

a lifetime of inattentiveness, too many toy cars on the floor.
How many saints cried out from here? You could probably
count them on one hand! The five amigos. Five fields

of clover, arrested development. He made you, too;
His hand on the twitch of your shoulder: so kind you know
He's here—along with the rest of your ranging clan.

AUGUST 4—*HOLY HOUR.*

"When you are at My feet praying or meditating, why not be one in spirit with all the pure in heart who are praying and meditating? . . .

"Become humble enough to lose yourself in everyone else and eager enough for merits to seek to benefit by the merits of your brothers, since I permit this. I am the Father who has found a way to let His children get rich quickly. . . . My little girl, don't you see how poor you are?

". . . The suffering ones, the persecuted, the abandoned, those in exile and in prison, those who are martyred for My name's sake, the souls in ruined bodies who continue to bless Me, to serve Me, and to call Me with all their love to their very last breath? Unite with them so that you may lose nothing of all this."

Our weight will be no revelation to them. The weak
have always carried the strong. While we cringe after
our nothings, they find rest in their want. And they won't

hold it against you. They see clearly, that you are a child
who likes the shiny ornaments on a Christmas tree.
They know better than to ever complain. They are busy elsewhere,

the sweat of work that needs done. Their conversation won't
    overwhelm.
(They will laugh during permitted breaks, wipe their brows.)
Your contributions will be welcome: juggling bean sacks badly,

your comic efforts. (They will teach you dated fight songs.)
No joy is wasted there. It spreads through the people
like bobbing flowers—or winds which top off the sea.

(We'll be part of the deep!) Our muscle will be His. No tree
will move the scene without our knowing. (The lovely
dark storm over fields might wake the national grain!)

Your new friends, playing corn hole, limping, loosing
a bandage, maybe grabbing a beer; they will know you.
When it's time to carouse, they'll get you to your feet.

AUGUST 11—*HOLY HOUR.*

"... You interior wealth should shine through you and make even the outside beautiful. You have no right to bury My light. It is time that the King's secret reach from soul to soul so that the heart of the King will be better understood and loved.... My flames are like a prairie fire. They sweep along with torrential speed setting alight as they go...

"My child, outside and inside, let everything about you speak of Me, give Me, make Me understood among the ignorant, the baffled, the hungry, the fearful, and the suffering ones."

Can my flesh leap with the flowers? Can my step outdo
itself? What would that look like? The Marys
running breakneck from the tomb, this time laughing?

I suppose we must seize others—at Walmart; the freshness
of love: a joy not reserved for the watery brinks
of heaven! A high five for my Down's son as he pauses,

stops at the five dollar movie bin! Don't ask
me for a definition—God never finishes what He starts.
I can only be a roadling, playing Jude's slide whistle.

It's the only song that takes us, writes our direction.
Who would've thought we had so little, so marginal
a part, promenading down these nearly-polished aisles,

finding a cheap jazzy sherbet shirt, to regale
the rest of the day with—my Jude, teething our bits
of heaven's money? There's no time to lose in this palace.

His is no secret kingdom. It delivers open
spaces: two knights, charging, widening a queue,
maybe freeing a cashier from this—or Mount Purgatory.

AUGUST 18—*THERE WAS A QUESTION OF A SURGICAL OPERATION FOR ME.*

"Whatever happens, what does it matter? Since you are Mine, since you live in My love? And since your pathway on earth leads to everlasting life, let everything take you to it.

"Ask Me to go this last part of the journey side by side with you. Make it the most intimate and the most joyous, since we'll be going at the same pace. You have your marching song—the will of God. No other song can raise your spirit like that one. We'll sing it together."

Life is sweet until He starts walking around, closing windows.
And then what do we have—what's left of our lives!
Another trek through dark trees, some standing water.

The winds will be more insistent this time, the voices,
not yours. But that pain is not your master yet.
And what will you say when it comes: "I wanted door

number two"? Today waits like a glistening unopened package.
That image means you'll probably be saved. So it's
our job to attend, to lose distractions. And hey,

this is The End, after all, Who's walking beside you!
He can't go anywhere—He's not! He's like a handful
of raisins, or the sun in a breakfast nook, His robe

trailing over the cracking grapevines out back. He inhales
flowers just to stir up the pollen. He never does
what you expect! I want my life to cry out

until only He can hear me. Rip open heaven,
O Wounded Surgeon. This violence will have your face!
And so what if He knocks over some furniture along the way?

AUGUST 25—

"If you are weary, rest. But take this rest on my heart.... And since this is for you, don't be afraid to accept it.... Offer My merits to the Father as if they were your very own....

"My merits never come to an end. They are fitted to everyone's need. They only multiply as you take them. For My merits are Myself."

His heart is an ocean. He's the rock and sway of things
as they are, a call that answers a restless self—
Your hammock on the sea. This is a swell that names you.

Each movement is new, each day invents itself,
like the trunk beneath your berth, sliding a little,
this way then that. You know this ship won't last

forever. Many of your friends are already gone.
The rest will follow. Today mostly takes care of itself.
It's a moment, settling as they never quite do—on the sea.

The heart of God is all you can get, offer.
There is too much noise in the other, larger world,
a place where nothing much ever seems to get done.

Better to stand where your feet won't be enough.
Better to learn old sea shanties. (You're never
alone, no matter the deep tombs, the peaks, the crests.)

The sea here is like His heart, supporting us.
He's the wet boards we walk on, the give and the take.
His wind, His sails, brother—everything is enough.

SEPTEMBER 8—*AT THE HOSPITAL AFTER AN OPERATION.*

"I could have come for you, couldn't I? And you would have let yourself be taken joyously. But you still want to do a little work for My glory, don't you? Gaily too? Isn't it true that nothing is worth living for except service for Me? . . .

"Together we'll weave the last threads of your life-pattern.

"When you feel weak as you do today, take your brother's power to love, to praise, to thank our Father. Don't deprive Him of any smile. A smile is a happy amen."

Obedient or not, the great river takes its toll.
Painful, late waters, where we'll grog, drift on our backs.
(So many tall trees will take in our final weaknesses!)

We'll each have to do our part, lie there in a bed,
or curl like a drying sidewalk grub, however
that comes—again. (My wife's dear face won't help.)

We will try to say yes. (It's the time that will be demanded.)
Jesus tells us to take a brother's power if need be:
the Little Flower maybe, someone who's suffered

better, in her ruined, gangrene-laced body—to offer
that with both hands, as if her strain could save us.
(And it will, though we cannot know that yet.) Sometimes

there is no out. We'll suffer because we are part
of the solution. Our happy face will strain, even
as she cradles the traces. She will help me persevere.

We cannot do this alone. We'll come in for a (mostly) choppy landing—a little bumpy, from our phrenological heads, down to the shake in our pale, knobby toes!

SEPTEMBER 15 — *CONVALESCENT. HOLY HOUR.*

"Let your return to life be a return to love. . . .

"The law of love is to keep on growing. Don't you feel a burning regret for the little that you give Me for all that I have given you? This fire that sometimes torments you is love itself. You must accept its torments and its joy, for to long for one or the other is the same as to long for love. Don't limit your longings. . . . Ask for this thirst, beg for it, let it be part of your life."

My spiritual director washed the little aristocrats,
my smooth feet, one Holy Thursday. Returning
to life must be something like that! After all, whom

have I loved well enough (from my closet cloister)? How focused,
eager have been my burning attentions? These
are the things that mark us, friend: what we aren't!

What do we bring to the next world, after all? Our inchings,
onward, pulled back—we want to save others from the us
we're in danger of becoming. (Who can help the palsied hand?

The palsied other—though who of us can ever
get this straight? (Let our basement laughter define us, what You
will do. We're unrepeatable, beautiful thugs.) With clumsy

hands we try to plant seeds, feel cartoonish,
wincing upward—as we wedge our squished little heads into joyful,
rocky creases. One eye narrows—then the next,

each squinting, prying upward. We push earth aside, seeking the pressure that defines us. We want to close the distance between God and ourselves. Our lives, an unrelenting jig.

SEPTEMBER 22—*THE PRIEST CAME TO HEAR MY CONFESSION IN MY SICKROOM.*

"... You needed this new unfolding of My love, didn't you ... all my kind attentions? .... Aren't they always new? So it is with My grace. You might think that it was always the same, but the truth is just as the sun, at every instant, sends out the right ray for the delicate posture of the flower, so there flows from Me to you exactly what you need for each passing moment."

This could be her death, only a year away:
the Last Rites, the help she'll get from another room.
Each chair will be different, one sliding across the floor.

The face of the next priest will be new—a rose.
Gabrielle will touch him, as we do, altering his walk,
how he'll say his next Mass. The Host rises, and each world

cracks itself wide open all over again.
Whatever face your heaven had simply cannot last,
because mercy changes us. He waits to become a room,

a grumpy nurse. He widens us. When we break down,
it's like a bridal announcement. We'll hear what seems
very like applause. (Saints are a ready lot.)

This is why water drips from the roof. This is why today
comes wrapped in the package it does. It's His statement—though
      I'll probably
lose too much of that when a wind rattles

my shutters!) But that will not stop Him. The sun will hit
your eye at just the right angle. It's enough to help
you catch a small movement, His bright left sleeve.

SEPTEMBER 29—*CONVALESCENCE*.

"You see the difference, don't you, between the life you offered Me before the trial and the one you want to offer Me now? Wasn't it good for you to feel yourself approaching the end of life so that you could see in the full light of reality the difference between life on earth and eternal life?

Now we shall no longer leave each other. I close your life in on all sides. I am your globe. If you burn, it is My fire. Your footsteps are mine. I am your breathing."

It's like going into a sunlit bar, one with several rocky
cataracts, the occasional lynx, where high snows open—
easy, celestial; a place with marbled pillars,

Olympian service—where everything you were was preamble!
The large spruce will help you to prioritize. And when the next
      stranger
walks into the room, he'll be Jesus. You'll think of the people

you carry with you! You'll want to smooth the blankets
of every bed, buy some cantaloupe. You'll want to heap
up fabric like heaven. You'll gird yourself (and your angel)

for the rest of the journey. Coins will make funny noises
on the floor, though people will be fine with your minor
      dependencies.
They'll know you're not finished yet. But could you ever be?

Your breathing is His. The end of your life seems close
enough to live. You're in heaven's courtyard again:
overhanging green leaves could be the tongues of angels,

the creaking gate that has always been there. This life
prepares us, doesn't it? It's a house we've always lived in.
I want to walk in Jesus, His days—His apples.

OCTOBER 6—*I WAS TRYING TO HOLD BACK SOMEONE WHO WAS BEING CARRIED AWAY BY A TERRIBLE PASSION.*

"You can't succeed alone. Call My mother. She will see Me in this man. She will take hold of him. But pray.

"How much you need to ask for the salvation of souls. All your little unused minutes—give them to Me for your brothers in danger. Be one with those who pray on the earth like a society of souls that draws its strength from Me.

"Be like God. Always strive to be the faithful image of Himself that He sketched in creating you."

They come, gathering rifles, translucent hats
(those small mumbling arguments we can still have with ourselves).
They're Mary's tattered soldiers, trying to forget

the clothes they wear. They have what the poor have always
had: their mother. You can see them begin to coalesce
in the dawn—take hold. Others come, stretch against the sky.

They have value, number. Birds appear in a pale,
morning moon. But this does not make them less important.
(The young have always contributed in startling ways.)

The force they have will be beyond you. This is so
every day. It's something only Jesus can see, flickering
shock troops creating a change in the field, in its color,

density. (God delights in sustaining the outcasts.)
You might think that this is World War One, but rather,
it's the skirmish behind: Our Lady, soon on a hill,

surrounded by sheep, children. Every soldier knows the tale,
in whichever direction they're walking, to this world—or the next!
They are that part of innocence which fills the earth!

OCTOBER 13—*HOLY HOUR*.

"My dear Christ, once again I've fallen into the same pride and the same selfishness."

"Why are you astonished, My child? Hasn't your life always been one continual beginning again? I love you this way, humbled, but ready to do better for love of Me. It's then that I come to your help. And the Spirit fills you because your eyes are open to your own worthlessness, and empty of self, you are ready at last to let Him take complete possession of you.

"Take My mother into your confidence. She'll help you keep watch. It will be easier with both of you, won't it?"

You could sing your songs across a stone-age bridge,
be a Templar—were it not for the coming age; trees
would spread wider. You could count on a hardier

species, yield. There was only one answer then.
(Our task has always been the same, though the distance
to it was less.) Shall we speak Medieval Latin

then, work that way? One had limited space
in those earlier days, granted, but an earl or sheriff
would always set you straight. (Maybe that's what

it's like to become British. I could learn manners, offer
baseball—enjoyment depends upon whom you're with.
And just like that, the world would be better.)

Mary would approve, nod her un-silent head.
I might detect the thwack of a bass line as
I walk down a New York street; I'd have a little

sunlit leafy patch with the God of the universe.
I might learn to crease the wind, like sidewalk flowers,
live in native, thoroughly out-dated Canarsee ways.

OCTOBER 20 — *HOLY HOUR.*

"Lord, my perseverance slips away like sand between my fingers."
  "Aren't you a poor little girl? Should your weakness astonish you?
Don't you see that you must give Me your hand continually? That you
must call me and accept the joy I bring? Joy is power. Sing in your heart.
That's the way you should go to meet a sacrifice—singing."
— Beers with my Adult Autistic Son

Our grown-up children, they break our hearts—that only
good in us. This is how they help us live our lives,
know theirs. Yesterday I watched some play-off hockey

with my beautiful son at a bar. His troubles, gains,
helped to bear me, as every growing child does—
alive. (Jesus gave this to me, so completely, off-handedly!)

The gift came with the ranging talk, how he rides Joseph,
his three-year-old on his river kayak, about
his horrible IT job: the breakage that makes

every man's life worthwhile. This was Jesus's "yes"
to me, a transparency my teenage aspy son
had never felt free enough to share. I gather

those moments like the pearls they are, late given. Could I know
a better road than that: simple, gravel-bedded?
He read me the whole blessed book. The beer helped, of course.

What father wouldn't rejoice to see the Lord act,
to see his own spiritual poverty help change his son?
What father wouldn't enjoy the walk back to his car?

OCTOBER 25 — (*ON THE TERRACE.*)

"Don't be like the October butterflies that can't fly anymore because
it's autumn and the wind is intractable. As your life goes on, go higher,
even higher."

Autumn is the sharpest time of the year, a pointed
statement. Joy comes easily, like old leaves,
because they don't have quite so far to go!

Imaginary terraces first appeared in childhood: huge places
for leaves, personal detachment, for un-annointed kings.
Distance had safety, a flare (kind of like it does now).

We walked, robed, next to a younger Jesus, who held us
in good stead. The larger seasons have never mattered.
One day can still save us, give us both wings and sound—

the paper-thin flutter, though our effort could still improve.
The old Pope has room on the piazza for us. A saint
happily goes fishing. A simple walk in the butterfly

garden might well change our lives. And so we power
through October, rinse our clothes in a bright stream.
Birds fly up—as autumn itself does, the days

left to us. Perhaps one of them will help us get this right.
Grandparents and children, up to our elbows in this world;
suds, the lives before us, larger than their cries.

OCTOBER 27—HOLY HOUR. IN MY BEDROOM.

"When I see that you are looking for Me, do you think I'm going to run away? When you call Me anxiously, won't I answer? Have I changed from the God I was in the first mornings of creation? . . .

"And since the Man-God allowed Himself to be crucified in cruel torture for your sake, don't I see Him still in each one of you?"

The Father is only hugely apprehended! We get Him
through an expansive verbal ease. Eight billion syllables,
the soul nebula are a drop in His oaken bucket.

He is like a memory you wish you had! He doesn't
mind your perturbations, spreading seed to His chickens.
He negotiates with them, promising good weather for eggs,

ranges for roaming. (No arbiter is in trouble at this table!)
His porch is large. He likes to rock His mammoth
wooden chair at sunset, its creak as He waits for His day

to settle. At night He stands tall, stretches (out loud).
"Tomorrow will be better," He says, patting your shoulder
as He gathers, slides past you. . . . When He's gone, He's not.

Things are just a little quieter. (What kind of night clouds
do you favor, my friend?) He needs you like an earth father
needs his children: their patter, the exciting variations.

We delight in His boldness, though we have to wonder, does
He enjoy His room, plans, commune with the moon?
(His stomp is beyond us, the first creational arc.)

NOVEMBER 3—*HOLY HOUR.*

... *"Lord, I have loved You so long, but I don't know yet how to love You."*
   "To love the Father and the Spirit, borrow My heart, and to love your Christ, offer Him His passion."

It's like we're on a long walk carrying a pie,
or a small bag full of second-hand toys. Your boots
are shiny, black. But you only get to wear them

three times a year. You have to smile, thinking
of elves, the big-headed children. This sleigh can fly
(the blue planet, like the marbled eye of God)!

It gives you time to think: the cost of Your love,
its size, color, in awkward tropical birds;
in the rain forest each species lifts its head,

reacts to our descending bells. And I wonder, which world
am I even in? I've never seen an angel—
probably because there's no need. The toys are enough.

Grace rules, though you sometimes feel the product of your senses.
You try to keep moving through the vagaries. Why complain?
Not everyone gets to ride a top-of-the-line

old classic. I mean, what would you rather be doing?
At one house, tonight, for example, someone placed
a carnation on a pillow (the faint smell of bubble gum).

NOVEMBER 10 — *HOLY HOUR.*

"Lord, there always seems to be a thick curtain between You and me, that hinders me from running to You."

"Fix it firmly in your mind that this presence of Me in you is not an allegory or a fantasy or a metaphor. It's not a story you listen to or something that might have happened to someone else. It has to do with you and Me. It has to do with a reality to be lived.

"Then live with assurance and gladness. You will find so much happiness in this and you will give Me so much joy. Greet Me in you often in your own way, in all sorts of ways. I'll love you in every one of these ways of yours.

. . . .

"The saints live for Me alone."

It's a gift you never expected, a camel down main street,
a lovely, bumpy ride. And where do you tie him
up outside of Burger King? (And what about

the long-term? Vet bills, food? Do you keep him
in or next to the garage?) Each lope around the block
i.d.'s you, though the kids, adults, eventually become friendly.

You have to give him a name: Cisco. And then
you figure, why put pressure on yourself? Things are what they are;
God wouldn't give you something without a way to carry on.

Besides, you've heard that someone across town has a zebra.
And you come to appreciate the awkwardness of your situation. It's how
we come, in our way. (God's love!) We can learn laughter!

We can learn how to polish our Sunday shoes. (In His radiance!)
I can see some friends on Sunday afternoons, crack open
a few. The King of Strange has been here forever.

He's been through each change, gave Bogart his middle name:
DeForrest! The man was a joyful Christmas baby,
a noir hero who invented the skift: snow!

NOVEMBER 17—*HOLY HOUR.*

"Why do I ask you to pray? Because prayer is to grace as the lighted match is to a candle.... God and man working together.... Wouldn't you find greater joy in hastening our reunion by your calling desires and your cries of love?...

"So don't be reticent....

"... And what can be said of those who have helped others know Me? The missionaries, the preachers, the writers? They will find, as it were, two banquets—theirs and that of their beneficiaries."

The call is always a response, a function of growth.
It's in the echo of the Sound who made us, candles
rewriting stories in dark rooms. Edison walked there.

Who wouldn't wave that delicate white tongue over
the barbaric roofs of the world? That's why we come.
God insists on our takes: the zippo factory, incense,

thuribles, candles. He plays, dances in every skirt
of wax, tells us that only virtue endures.
(And so what if we walk slower than we would like.)

We can hear Hopkins's birds sing, insistent mornings.
There's nothing but days like this ahead of us.
I could meet you, new friend, on the road; we'd be like a couple

of cronies under mottled leaves—no way to talk yet.
We could stand there, wait for a wave of conversation.
The first moves (concern for the other) do the most to heal us,

so faint that we might feel our thinnest shells
start to crack, break open. Every missionary work
begins at home. And home? That's somewhere else.

DECEMBER 1—*HOLY HOUR.*

"Have you forgotten that is it your weakness that attracts your
God? . . . Don't be like the silent ones who consider themselves too
unworthy to ask for magnificent favors. . . . Be like the humble ones
who expose their poverty and count on their Christ to transform them
at each Confession, because He hears their cry of regret and turns it
into a hymn for His glory."

I want the faith of Christian lions. I want
bear cubs to play-fight inside me. I want high river salmon,
the unspoiled reigning toss of high limbs, waterfalls.

When I make a loud noise, I want to hear cracking trees.
I want my young neighbors—alive! Who could know what they
    think?
I watch them with spade, wheelbarrow. They're always doing
    Whitman

without knowing it, or defter Betjeman, with his smaller
Anglican inquiries. (Where *are* we when none of us
can see what's broken? On the other hand, perhaps

that's the thing that gives us voice!) We all cry out—
in wonder. Let me count my pieces. Let me see You moving
in each of our stunted friends. We are rough-hewn saints.

There's always room in Your ruined monasteries, where we
can be those bear cubs, know the feel of open air.
Your quiet invented the sacraments—God-food and monstrance!

Saws in Merton's forest! You're a collector of weaknesses.
We can walk through the trees with our crotalus, clap for the dead:
those parts of us, moving too slowly—might come alive.

DECEMBER 8—*HOLY HOUR.* FEAST OF THE IMMACULATE CONCEPTION.

"Why don't you offer everything by the hands of your mother, by her sorrowful and immaculate heart today and in your living and your dying? You know that she loves those two titles because I gave her first her very pure conception, then suffering for the greater part of her life. And everything that God gave her she received so very humbly with love and respect.... Give yourself to Mary so that you may walk in her ways.... she knows you in your difficulties, almost all of which come from human pride.

"Draw the curtain across your interior stage.... Come to me to buy perfect love, for I possess it.... for this love of yours is My joy."

"[I]n ... your dying" stays with us, because in one year
that will come. How delicately He prepares her! That and "suffering
for the greater part" and "with respect." Though I must

admit, I've never been keen for that particular embrace.
Our Lady, of course, will make me new. It's His heart
she still carries, after all—and His pain: I remember curling

on an Austrian hospital bench, my wife, trying
to get me admitted. (I thought of people centuries
before: no pain killers, the hours of extended agony

before death. How did they endure?) I didn't feel Mary's
presence. He didn't allow that. Only the cross.
(If He wills a thing, that's enough. I say that now—

and a little then.) Mary, take my weak hand.
Remember how I caught the cold in Lourdes water!
Give me the only gift that matters: humility—

I'll disappear when I catch the flush of your farmyard face.
What words will you say, around what heavenly stile?
Enough to make me at home; people fresh as eggs.

DECEMBER 9—FEAST DAY OF ST. JUAN DIEGO.

"Couldn't you put an end to all these little useless thoughts that do nothing for you or your neighbor or God, and substitute others. . . . All of this would be like the plants that brighten up reception rooms."

The suggestions get pointed, the closer she gets to death.
We are all convicted—but in this morning's reading,
Mark 4: 30–34, Jesus mentions

"parables" three times. It's the poetic way we work out
our salvation. I gave you your imagination, He says,
to figure things out as you go, Eustice (Lewis).

You can see this as we hold up each wayward thought,
a muddy eel or huge slug by its tail. Alive,
the heavy thing muscles in the sun, shiny blue, black—

its sway, desire, as it attempts to re-gather, keep on.
Perhaps an Inkling or Our Lady could help with a story.
How much work we need to do, how deeply we

must settle, childlike, next to Juan Diego.
A good part of us wants to eel, to slither away.
(But the river we are must have enough verve, movement,

to create a shore.) Its riot is gift, as we
enliven—ourselves! Like Tepeyac, our feet must pad
the forest, spelling us as we run to the bishop's house.

DECEMBER 11 —*END OF THE NOVENA TO THE IMMACULATE. I WAS DEEPLY MOVED BY THE MASS SUNG IN FIVE PARTS.*

"What will you say in heaven when you hear My praises sung in billions of parts? Each of the blessed ones has his own particular melody."

Harmonies can only be woven through disparate threads,
which is why "My praises sung" sounds odd to us!
(It's that sense of God-Self that Jesus brings to the text.)

Either way, our moments will one day be seen as context,
a provisional I am, waves reaching out before
they never really close, provide an answer. (The song

of the people—a sea.) Today, we mostly only hear
the flute, the sounds that skip across stones, or water.
The birds sing, the trees actively hushing in the background.

I come here to be known, Jesus, to call with each breath
I take, even the last. We can't help ourselves.
This is both praise and articulation. Neighbors are friends

because they're so far from us. (The gap must close,
brother, then open again. Our calls tell us that.)
We'll hear what's already here, what partially coheres

and moves us past ourselves. How can that ever
be different, though we will get all of it there: the sounds
of the Three, rippling, each splash, all answers contending.

DECEMBER—*I WAS HEARING OF THE ENTHUSIASTIC REMARKS BY READERS OF* **LUI ET *MOI* (HE AND I.)**

"Thank you, Lord, for all these choice graces you are scattering about in secret."

"You don't know them all. Only in heaven will you learn about them and what joy will that be for you!

". . . Even the desire to come nearer to Me brings my heart ease. An upsoaring of love, however momentary in the midst of your activities, pleases Me. And if one of you reaches the point of living for Me alone, I heap that one with favors in this life, for he offers Me a refuge on earth. But don't imagine that there are many like that.

"Read the gospels."

The leaves fall in both worlds. We love You with a love
You give. And who could repay the little we've known!
(Yes, Jesus. And Jesus again.) The cause at our fingertips

and the world we rouse. I would like to see people more clearly—
our speaking God. He is here, always. Writers
can help me see that: Bossis, Eliot, Dante,

R. S. Thomas, Mackay Brown. Let the bells ring
in wet leaves, pages leafing the garden's stories.
Thanks again, for You (though the rest is carnage, a scarring

world destroying itself. The churning of fodder—
bodies. It's grim tilled soil, rolling back, over
itself. We look: millions of innocent crosses).

Everything, even now, is being made new, if we see
that or not. This is about who He is and nothing
else! The One who finally gives us form

and its meaning, the One whose hand we raise when we raise
our own. The words may seem ours, but He's the One
who speaks in swirling leaves—in the settling after.

DECEMBER 15 — HOLY HOUR.

Coming back from Mass in the dark at 7 am in the freezing rain. "This, too, Lord, may I offer for Your sinners of this Marian year?"
　　"You forget your past sufferings, but they continue to bear fruit in My sight. You have already forgotten your travel weariness, weather annoyances, desert thirst, the fears, exile in distant countries, the slow journeys back, the long tests of endurance, times of illness. But remember that you offered Me everything and that I've kept everything
　　"... I have found joy in all the little presents given to Me by My children."

God bless His memory, the One who gathers good
as if only that mattered. He's like a dad. Who, after
all, would round up mementos of his children's sorrows:

the ball game blow-outs, soiled bandages? He is sweetness
Itself, the orange in that fruit. When we're in His house,
which is always, His is the music we play! If the gramophone

scratches, we can buy a needle, participate; we can go
outside, walk the porch rail. There's no stasis here.
Whatever you thought you knew is wrong. (This is

what happens when you live in the present! You're a father's delight:
a lessoned youth, an error in the glorious making.)
Look for more shortcomings if you must, the only thing

you'll run into is all you don't know. Best to round up
those closest, gather yourself around a friendly table.
You can find your place in the time already come.

The last bits of self-destruction, of course, must be shaved—
heaven finishing its task. It's been around for a while,
you know, making its list, writing names down twice!

DECEMBER 22—*HOLY HOUR*.

"Lord, may nothing in me hinder Your voice from reaching others."
"Echo it back with all your loving warmth and you will give them joy. And this very joy will make them much more sensitive to My voice, these poor people, so often troubled with regard to Me or consumed by earthly worries. How much more freely will they breathe if you talk with them about Me.

". . . It's like a cherished secret that you disclose because you can no longer keep it. It's as though you said, 'Let us talk about God, the one who is my entire life, the one who alone is worthy of my every heartbeat.'

"Oh, when evening falls may they think of coming to My embrace, their hearts overflowing with gratitude, asking Me to come again with new blessings. And I will come again. And in this way we shall approach the end of life and the last of My blessings.

"For this last blessing, My child, give Me your tender thanks now."

—AFTER A CONVERSATION WITH BILL N.

When Living Water, an end, finds Its surprising place,
It raises the conversation. (The rocks are part of the show,
holding up cold mountain streams with steady arms.)

More gets said so quickly, that you, too, are surprised.
(And then He passes, both parties changed.) You both
recognize that flash of genius Who, for that moment,

had taken His rightful stage. It's what poems can do
at their best. (Only You can spell Your name!) We live
along ruffling banks, where everything alive moves happily

to its end. On some days we can walk around like that.
This is how creativity finds itself, kneaded in God's hands.
(You become enraptured, almost as if you were playing pong

in a college basement bar again.) This talk
about Jesus! When can you do that again? Most times
we are elsewhere, so we have to let the chance find us.

(May Bill and his family be blessed, under the first tree!)
Orange or palm! Let there be a plate of dates
or olives among friends, some weightier, more personal matters!

DECEMBER 29— . . .

"Lord, I should so love to put into practice all that You have told me. Instead of running, I'm dragging along."

"Do you remember this sentence: 'The weight of your favors has been part of my burden?' This is because the more I give, the more clearly you see your wretchedness, and this is the light of reality. . .

". . . Those who are thirsty never stop asking for a drink. Are you saddened by your usual mediocrity? If you weren't, how could I help you? . . . So learn, learn to cry to Me, My child."

This is where most of us live, surrounded by spent toys,
forever unsatisfied children of a King. And poetry's
no answer. (That's just a means to harness the end!)

We live against our betters, listening languages we never
completely understand. One day things will be different.
We'll have their cheerful company, heavenly hobos—

we'll finally have a place to lay our heads.
At night, we'll be able to raise our eyes, sitting next to
Dante, Shakespeare, Harvey Kuenn, my old

baseball friend from 92nd street, a catcher
on the local teen team. Nothing will be missing:
stars, a game a street over. The King will rule

His world of owls, bats, the moon (with lockers
for the disabled). May our poetry help. Poor gifts are best;
they mirror the only part of us that matters: our hearts.

May they patiently beat as You change every old place—
two mutts in uniform, standing in a porch-step photo.
Every experience will finally reveal itself!

www.ingramcontent.com/pod-product-compliance
Lightning Source LLC
Chambersburg PA
CBHW061454040426
42450CB00007B/1350